**SCHOLASTIC**

# Critical Thinking
# Card Games

Reproducible, Easy-to-Play Card and Board Games That Build
Kids' Critical Thinking Skills — and Help Them Succeed on Tests

bright ideas™
**from
Elaine Richard**

NEW YORK • TORONTO • LONDON • AUCKLAND • SYDNEY
MEXICO CITY • NEW DELHI • HONG KONG • BUENOS AIRES

**Teaching**
*Resources*

# Dedication

These games are dedicated to:

all the children who worked with me over the
past 20 years to acquire good critical-thinking skills;

my three grandchildren—Katie, Sam, and Jake—
who played these games with me just for the fun of it;

the teachers, tutors, and parents dedicated to helping
every student achieve to the highest;

Andrea and Mark for their patient and indispensable computer tutoring;

and, of course, to Jack, for his patience, advice, and encouragement.

Cover and interior design by Holly Grundon
Illustrations by Kelly Kennedy

ISBN 0-439-66542-6
Copyright © 2005 by Elaine Richard
All rights reserved.
Printed in the U.S.A.

2 3 4 5 6 7 8 9 10      40      12 11 10 09 08 07 06 05

# Contents

Introduction . . . . . . . . . . . . . . . . . . . . . . . . . . . . 5

Think About It. . . . . . . . . . . . . . . . . . . . . . . . . 7
Riddle Me Silly . . . . . . . . . . . . . . . . . . . . . . . . 14
Play Your Hunch. . . . . . . . . . . . . . . . . . . . . . 19
How Can You Tell? . . . . . . . . . . . . . . . . . . . 25
Fact or Opinion. . . . . . . . . . . . . . . . . . . . . . 30
Reading Between the Lines . . . . . . . . . . . . . 35
You've Got to Be Kidding! . . . . . . . . . . . . . 42
Classified. . . . . . . . . . . . . . . . . . . . . . . . . . . 47
Making Connections. . . . . . . . . . . . . . . . . . 54
Let's Compare . . . . . . . . . . . . . . . . . . . . . . . 59

Game Board A . . . . . . . . . . . . . . . . . . . . . . . 64
Game Board B . . . . . . . . . . . . . . . . . . . . . . . 66

Possible Answers. . . . . . . . . . . . . . . . . . . . . 68

# Introduction

To become truly accomplished, independent readers, children need to move beyond decoding and word knowledge, and develop critical thinking and reasoning skills. Honing these skills leads to better comprehension, which is the cornerstone of successful reading, understanding, and studying skills.

What better way to develop students' critical thinking and reasoning skills than through fun, easy-to-play games? Enter *10 Critical Thinking Card Games*! The games in this book help boost and reinforce essential reasoning skills—by giving children the kind of practice they'll enjoy doing over and over again. As children play these games, they get practice in making generalizations, solving riddles, predicting outcomes, distinguishing fact from opinion, recognizing inconsistencies, drawing conclusions, and more.

## Setting Up the Games

Most of the games require nothing more than the cards provided. (Two games, "Think About It" and "Play Your Hunch," come with their own game boards.) Simply photocopy the game cards on cardstock, cut them apart, and store them in a plastic zipper bag along with a copy of the game instructions. Label the bag with the name of the game and store the bag in a filing box for easy access.

For a slightly more competitive twist, we also provide two generic game boards that can be used with some of the card games. Let students decide which game board to use for a particular game. (You might even invite students to create their own game boards.) Photocopy the game boards on regular copy paper then glue the pages to the inside of a manila folder, carefully aligning both sides of the game board. You could also photocopy the game board on cardstock and tape the two sides together. Consider laminating the game boards or covering them with clear plastic to keep them clean and sturdy for repeated use.

## Playing the Games

The games in this book are designed for two to four players. A few can also be played at the board in a whole-class setting or in teams. You may want to establish some simple rules when you first introduce the games to avoid potential conflicts later on. For example, a quick solution to the question of who goes first is to have the youngest player always go first in a game, then play can move in a clockwise direction. A more traditional method would be to have players throw a number cube (or die) and the player with the highest number goes first. Then play continues in a clockwise direction.

Students might also play a game as "solitaire." In this case, the player writes the answers on a sheet of paper and hands it to you when he or she is finished. This could serve as an assessment tool to give you insight into the student's understanding.

Consider making the games part of the reading center or offering them as a choice during free time. You might also select a game to play with small reading groups, supervising the game to ensure appropriate answers. (Most of the games are open-ended and don't require exact answers. We provide possible answers for most games at the back of this book. You can photocopy the answer keys and give them to players to use for reference. Remind students that these are only possible answers. Accept any reasonable answers as long as players can justify them.)

Perhaps more effective than any of these options is to play the games in a one-on-one setting with an adult and a student, especially if the student needs extra help in any of the skills. A parent, teacher, or tutor can model more precise or interesting answers than peers might. Consider sending home copies of the games so students can play them with their families—another great way to strengthen the home–school connection.

However you decide to use the games in this book, they're sure to provide lots of fun and learning. Enjoy!

# Think About It!

> **Given open-ended questions, players try to come up with as many logical answers as possible.**

## Objective

To give students practice in drawing conclusions, using experience and logical thinking

## Players

2 to 4 players

## You'll Need

- 8 Think About It cards (choose from pages 8–11)
- Think About It game board (pages 12–13)
- Paper and pencil for each player
- Number cube (die)
- Timer (optional)

## How to Play

**1.** Place one card on each cabin on the game board. Distribute paper and pencils to each player.

**2.** Starting at the first cabin, a player rolls the number cube to determine how many answers to give for the question. For example, if a player rolls a 5, each player must list five possible answers to the question. (You may want to use a timer and set a time limit, like 30 seconds or 1 minute.)

**3.** Play continues as players move to the next cabin and repeat step 2.

**4.** After everyone has gone through all the cabins, players compare answers for each question. Cross out any answers that are the same as other players'. Decide as a group which of the remaining answers are logical and count them. The player with the most number of logical answers wins.

10 Critical Thinking Card Games    Scholastic Teaching Resources

**1** Think About It

What can you
do in winter but
not in summer?

**2** Think About It

What do ice and
steam have
in common?

**3** Think About It

What can you do on
the weekend but not
on a school day?

**4** Think About It

What do you swallow
but not chew?

**5** Think About It

Who can you recognize
from very far away?

**6** Think About It

What can a person
do only once or
twice in his life?

**7** Think About It

What job could keep
you in good shape?

**8** Think About It

What costs less
today than it did
10 years ago?

**9** Think About It

What is sometimes too
short for a tall person?

**10** Think About It

What do you
always have more
than one of?

**11** Think About It

What can you identify
by its smell?

**12** Think About It

What can you identify
by its shape?

**13** Think About It

What food tastes better fresh than canned?

**19** Think About It

What should be done very carefully?

**14** Think About It

What would you like to keep all your life?

**20** Think About It

What should be cooked before it is eaten?

**15** Think About It

What can change shape?

**21** Think About It

What looks different when it is wet than when it is dry?

**16** Think About It

What has a right side and a wrong side?

**22** Think About It

What would you not wash in a washing machine?

**17** Think About It

What gets loaded and unloaded?

**23** Think About It

What is easy to remember?

**18** Think About It

What would you put at the bottom of a grocery bag?

**24** Think About It

What is difficult to remember?

**25** Think About It

What are some things money cannot buy?

**26** Think About It

What should you not do with dirty hands?

**27** Think About It

How is a doctor different from a nurse?

**28** Think About It

What can a computer do that a person cannot do?

**29** Think About It

How is a kitchen different from a dining room?

**30** Think About It

How is a peach different from a banana?

**31** Think About It

What does a stew have that a steak doesn't have?

**32** Think About It

What can a person do that a dog cannot do?

**33** Think About It

What can a dog do better than a person?

**34** Think About It

How is a college different from a high school?

**35** Think About It

How are a watch and a clock different?

**36** Think About It

What can the President do that a mayor cannot do?

**37** Think About It

How can you tell a rose from a daffodil?

**43** Think About It

How is flossing different from brushing your teeth?

**38** Think About It

What do you start but often don't finish?

**44** Think About It

What stays cold all summer?

**39** Think About It

What goes out but never leaves its home?

**45** Think About It

What follows you everywhere?

**40** Think About It

Where would you most often hear a siren?

**46** Think About It

Why is water important?

**41** Think About It

What would you hear near a roller coaster?

**47** Think About It

Why is a hurricane dangerous?

**42** Think About It

What is lighter than air?

**48** Think About It

What do you see in the evening but not during the day?

Scholastic Teaching Resources

48 Critical Thinking Card Games

# Think About It

# Riddle Me Silly

**Players use critical thinking to figure out answers to riddles.**

## Objective

To expose students to riddles, humor, double meanings, and playful language

## Players

2 to 4 players

## You'll Need

- Riddle Me Silly cards (pages 15–18)

## Optional Materials

- Game board (choose one from pages 64–67)
- Game markers (buttons or coins work well)
- Number cube (die)

## How to Play

1. Shuffle the "Riddle Me Silly" cards and stack them facedown between the players.

2. On each player's turn, the person to the right of the player picks a card and reads the riddle aloud. The player then has to figure out the answer to the riddle.

3. If the player answers correctly, she keeps the card. If not, the reader reads the answer and places the card in a discard pile. The next player takes a turn.

4. Play continues until no cards are left. Players then count how many cards they've collected. The player with the most cards at the end of the game wins.

## Playing With a Game Board

Each player places a marker on START. Play the game as described above. If a player answers correctly, she rolls the number cube to see how many spaces to move along the board. If the player doesn't answer correctly, she cannot move. Place used cards in a discard pile. The next player takes a turn. The first player to reach FINISH wins.

10 Critical Thinking Card Games    Scholastic Teaching Resources

## Riddle Me Silly

**1.** What has four legs but only one foot?

(A bed)

**2.** What bird helps you eat?

(A swallow)

**3.** Why do birds fly south in winter?

(It's too far to walk.)

**4.** What room is never part of a house?

(A mushroom)

**5.** What does someone have to take before you get it?

(Your photograph)

**6.** What state is round at both ends but "hi" in the middle?

(Ohio)

**7.** What word is always pronounced wrong?

(Wrong)

**8.** What do you lose every time you stand up?

(Your lap)

**9.** What has teeth but never bites?

(A comb)

**10.** What animal keeps the best time?

(A watch dog)

**11.** What odd number becomes even when you remove the first letter?

(Seven)

**12.** What has a head and tail but no body?

(A coin)

**13** Riddle Me Silly

Where do frogs
keep their money?

(In a river bank)

**14** Riddle Me Silly

What falls often but
never gets hurt?

(Snow or rain)

**15** Riddle Me Silly

What kind of key
cannot open a lock?

(A monkey)

**16** Riddle Me Silly

If your nose runs and
your feet smell, what's
wrong with you?

(You are upside down.)

**17** Riddle Me Silly

What never asks questions
but everyone answers it?

(The telephone)

**18** Riddle Me Silly

What kind of coat is
always put on wet?

(A coat of paint)

**19** Riddle Me Silly

What belongs to you but
others use it more often
than you do?

(Your name)

**20** Riddle Me Silly

When is the best time
to use a trampoline?

(When you feel jumpy)

**21** Riddle Me Silly

What gets broken every
time you say its name?

(Silence)

**22** Riddle Me Silly

What can a circle do
that a square can't?

(Look round)

**23** Riddle Me Silly

What 10-letter word
starts with gas?

(Automobile)

**24** Riddle Me Silly

What animal
doesn't play fairly?

(A cheetah)

**25** Riddle Me Silly

Why are fish easy to weigh?

(They have scales.)

**26** Riddle Me Silly

What can speak any language in the world?

(An echo)

**27** Riddle Me Silly

What has 16 legs and 4 tails?

(4 horses or any other four-legged animals with tails)

**28** Riddle Me Silly

What does a cat have that no other animal has?

(Kittens)

**29** Riddle Me Silly

Why did the two surgeons like to work together?

(They wanted to co-operate.)

**30** Riddle Me Silly

What has four wheels and flies?

(A garbage truck)

**31** Riddle Me Silly

What question can never be answered "yes"?

(Are you asleep?)

**32** Riddle Me Silly

How do you know that chefs are mean?

(They beat eggs and whip cream.)

**33** Riddle Me Silly

What did the crook get when he stole the calendar?

(30 days or 1 year)

**34** Riddle Me Silly

What goes up when rain comes down?

(An umbrella)

**35** Riddle Me Silly

What lets you see through walls?

(Windows)

**36** Riddle Me Silly

What kind of footwear can you make from banana peels?

(Slippers)

**37** Riddle Me Silly

Why was the baseball player arrested?

(He stole second base.)

**38** Riddle Me Silly

What do you call male cattle that are sleeping?

(Bull-dozers)

**39** Riddle Me Silly

How did the basketball court get so wet?

(The players dribbled a lot.)

**40** Riddle Me Silly

What do you call someone who is crazy about chocolate?

(A cocoa-nut)

**41** Riddle Me Silly

How do you know that robbers are very strong?

(They hold up banks.)

**42** Riddle Me Silly

Why does the ocean seem friendly?

(It waves.)

**43** Riddle Me Silly

Why did the postman get the sack?

(So he could carry the mail.)

**44** Riddle Me Silly

How do you make a bandstand?

(Take their chairs away.)

**45** Riddle Me Silly

In what month do people talk the least?

(February)

**46** Riddle Me Silly

What can you always count on?

(Your fingers)

**47** Riddle Me Silly

What is the difference between a canoe and a miser?

(A canoe tips a lot, but a miser doesn't.)

**48** Riddle Me Silly

What flowers do people always have with them?

(Tulips)

# Play Your Hunch

> **Players try to move from START to FINISH by matching a noun card with an appropriate verb on the game board.**

## Objective

To give students practice in using logic, critical thinking, and strategy

## Players

2 players, or 2 teams of 2 players each (This game can also be played as a solitaire activity—the player tries to get to FINISH in the fewest moves.)

## You'll Need

- Play Your Hunch cards (pages 20–23)
- 2 copies of the Words in Action game board (page 24)
- Game markers (buttons or coins work well)

## How to Play

1. Shuffle the "Play Your Hunch" cards and stack them facedown between the players. Each player gets a copy of the game board.

2. The object of the game is to move from START to FINISH by matching a card with a verb on the board. Players can move only one square at a time in any direction. On each turn, a player picks a card from the stack. The player must explain how the noun on the card relates to the verb in a logical way. (Note that some of the nouns are living things and some are nonliving things.) For example, if a player picks a card that says *radio*, he might say that the noun relates to the verb *hear* because you can hear a radio. If the other players agree, he can place his marker on top of the verb on his board. The next player takes a turn. Put the used card in a discard pile.

3. Play continues with players picking a card and trying to move through their own game board.

4. The first player to reach FINISH wins.

10 Critical Thinking Card Games    Scholastic Teaching Resources

| Play Your Hunch | Play Your Hunch | Play Your Hunch |
|---|---|---|
| book | paper | stairs |
| Play Your Hunch | Play Your Hunch | Play Your Hunch |
| car | pencil | cloth |
| Play Your Hunch | Play Your Hunch | Play Your Hunch |
| elevator | pen | ball |
| Play Your Hunch | Play Your Hunch | Play Your Hunch |
| hammer | bowl | needle |
| Play Your Hunch | Play Your Hunch | Play Your Hunch |
| stove | pot | soap |

| Play Your Hunch | Play Your Hunch | Play Your Hunch |
|---|---|---|
| coat | backpack | button |
| Play Your Hunch | Play Your Hunch | Play Your Hunch |
| string | bicycle | desk |
| Play Your Hunch | Play Your Hunch | Play Your Hunch |
| rope | hat | sofa |
| Play Your Hunch | Play Your Hunch | Play Your Hunch |
| bricks | chair | music |
| Play Your Hunch | Play Your Hunch | Play Your Hunch |
| spoon | pitcher | chalk |

| Play Your Hunch | Play Your Hunch | Play Your Hunch |
|---|---|---|
| frog | worm | monkey |
| Play Your Hunch | Play Your Hunch | Play Your Hunch |
| tiger | artist | snake |
| Play Your Hunch | Play Your Hunch | Play Your Hunch |
| lion | pianist | camel |
| Play Your Hunch | Play Your Hunch | Play Your Hunch |
| bear | butterfly | flower |
| Play Your Hunch | Play Your Hunch | Play Your Hunch |
| wolf | giraffe | fish |

| Play Your Hunch | Play Your Hunch | Play Your Hunch |
|---|---|---|
| boy | kitten | mosquito |
| Play Your Hunch | Play Your Hunch | Play Your Hunch |
| cow | canary | sister |
| Play Your Hunch | Play Your Hunch | Play Your Hunch |
| horse | dog | elephant |
| Play Your Hunch | Play Your Hunch | Play Your Hunch |
| shark | baby | tree |
| Play Your Hunch | Play Your Hunch | Play Your Hunch |
| father | bee | onion |

START

# Words in Action

| hear | stand | sew | eat | jump | build |
|------|-------|-----|-----|------|-------|
| ride | hop | fly | roar | hunt | play |
| color | shout | wash | tie | crawl | drive |
| sit on | dance | hide | cook | lift | paint |
| smell | read | write | talk | wear | swim |
| fix | smile | draw | throw | climb | carry |

*10 Critical Thinking Card Games*   Scholastic Teaching Resources

**FINISH**

# How Can You Tell?

**Players explain what event(s) might have led to the statement on each card.**

## Objective

To give students practice in drawing conclusions, and making inferences and generalizations

## Players

1 to 4 players (For a solitaire game, the player can write his or her answers on a piece of paper.)

## You'll Need

- How Can You Tell... cards (pages 26–29)

## Optional Materials

- Game board (choose one from pages 64–67)
- Game markers (buttons or coins work well)
- Number cube (die)

## How to Play

**1.** Shuffle the "How Can You Tell..." cards and stack them facedown between the players.

**2.** Players take turns picking a card from the pile. On each turn, a player reads aloud the question and answers it.

**3.** If the answer makes sense and the other players agree, the player can keep the card. If other players do not agree with the answer, the next player can offer an alternative answer. If the other players agree with this answer, he can keep the card and take another turn.

**4.** Continue taking turns until no cards are left. Players then count how many cards they've collected. The player with the most cards at the end of the game wins.

## Playing With a Game Board

Each player places a marker on START. Play the game as described above. If a player answers correctly, she rolls the number cube to see how many spaces to move along the board. If the player doesn't answer correctly, she cannot move. Place used cards in a discard pile. The next player takes a turn. The first player to reach FINISH wins.

10 Critical Thinking Card Games    Scholastic Teaching Resources

**1** How Can You Tell...

...the plant is going to die soon?

**2** How Can You Tell...

...the storm must have been very strong?

**3** How Can You Tell...

...the baby must be very tired?

**4** How Can You Tell...

...those crackers are stale?

**5** How Can You Tell...

...the meat is not yet cooked?

**6** How Can You Tell...

...the roses will bloom in a week or two?

**7** How Can You Tell...

...the floor needs sweeping?

**8** How Can You Tell...

...the soda is flat?

**9** How Can You Tell...

...the milk is sour?

**10** How Can You Tell...

...she had a tooth pulled?

**11** How Can You Tell...

...the cheese is spoiled?

**12** How Can You Tell...

...he's going to get a speeding ticket?

**13** How Can You Tell...

...Mom came home in a very good mood?

**19** How Can You Tell...

...the pencil needs sharpening?

**14** How Can You Tell...

...he must have run all the way to school?

**20** How Can You Tell...

...the plane just landed?

**15** How Can You Tell...

...the car has a flat tire?

**21** How Can You Tell...

...from a distance that the store is closed?

**16** How Can You Tell...

...the plant needs watering?

**22** How Can You Tell...

...your neighbor must be out of town?

**17** How Can You Tell...

...something is burning?

**23** How Can You Tell...

...your best friend has a cold?

**18** How Can You Tell...

...that person is very upset at the clerk?

**24** How Can You Tell...

...you will need your sunglasses today?

**25** How Can You Tell...

...the peach isn't ripe?

**26** How Can You Tell...

...I need a haircut?

**27** How Can You Tell...

...the hem needs to be sewn?

**28** How Can You Tell...

...someone must have hit the car?

**29** How Can You Tell...

...you'll have to take that photo over again?

**30** How Can You Tell...

...there must be a party at their house?

**31** How Can You Tell...

...the bus drivers must be on strike?

**32** How Can You Tell...

...it's going to snow tomorrow?

**33** How Can You Tell...

...that tree will have to be cut down?

**34** How Can You Tell...

...your mother is proud of you?

**35** How Can You Tell...

...the girl at the next table celebrated her birthday?

**36** How Can You Tell...

...I need new shoes?

**37** How Can You Tell...

...your friend must have been away to a sunny climate?

**38** How Can You Tell...

...she started taking piano lessons?

**39** How Can You Tell...

...the road is very icy?

**40** How Can You Tell...

...the cookies were baked too long?

**41** How Can You Tell...

...someone has lit a match?

**42** How Can You Tell...

...he wants to be your friend?

**43** How Can You Tell...

...the house needs painting?

**44** How Can You Tell...

...you're going to get a good mark on the test?

**45** How Can You Tell...

...the dog is very excited?

**46** How Can You Tell...

...you ate too much?

**47** How Can You Tell...

...you grew at least 2 inches over the summer?

**48** How Can You Tell...

...your dad is on a diet?

# Fact or Opinion

> **Players decide whether a sentence on a card is fact or opinion.**

## Objective

To give students practice in distinguishing between fact and opinion—what is true and what is believed

## Players

2 to 4 players

## You'll Need

- Fact or Opinion cards (pages 31–34)
- Game board (choose one from pages 64–67)
- Game markers (buttons or coins work well)
- Number cube (die)

## How to Play

**1.** Shuffle the "Fact or Opinion" cards and stack them next to the game board.

**2.** Players take turns picking a card from the pile. On each turn, a player reads aloud the sentence on the card and says whether it's a fact or an opinion.

**3.** If the player answers correctly, she rolls the number cube to see how many spaces to move on the game board. If the player doesn't answer correctly, she cannot move. Place the card in a discard pile. The next player takes a turn.

**4.** The first player to reach FINISH wins.

**1**    Fact or Opinion

New York City has
many tall buildings.

**2**    Fact or Opinion

Cows and sheep give milk.

**3**    Fact or Opinion

Candy is bad for your teeth.

**4**    Fact or Opinion

Sammy Sosa is the best
baseball player who ever lived.

**5**    Fact or Opinion

Applesauce is sweet.

**6**    Fact or Opinion

Peaches are the sweetest fruits.

**7**    Fact or Opinion

Carrots are healthier than candy.

**8**    Fact or Opinion

George Washington was
our first president.

**9**    Fact or Opinion

Football players and
wrestlers are mean.

**10**    Fact or Opinion

Exercise is good for you.

**11**    Fact or Opinion

It is best to get a good
night's sleep before a big test.

**12**    Fact or Opinion

The Pacific Ocean is on the
West Coast of the United States.

**13**   Fact or Opinion

Basketball is more fun than soccer.

**14**   Fact or Opinion

Hamburgers taste better than hot dogs.

**15**   Fact or Opinion

Alaska is bigger than North Carolina.

**16**   Fact or Opinion

Cars and motorcycles run on gasoline.

**17**   Fact or Opinion

My bike goes faster than yours.

**18**   Fact or Opinion

My sister is smarter than yours.

**19**   Fact or Opinion

Tractors make neat rows on farms.

**20**   Fact or Opinion

Farm horses live in barns.

**21**   Fact or Opinion

Red is a prettier color than blue.

**22**   Fact or Opinion

The cello is a difficult instrument to play.

**23**   Fact or Opinion

According to our survey, pizza is the most popular school lunch.

**24**   Fact or Opinion

Every classroom should have a computer.

**25** Fact or Opinion

We sing the national anthem before every Yankee game.

**31** Fact or Opinion

Going to the beach is more fun than going hiking.

**26** Fact or Opinion

Many kids like to eat in restaurants with their parents.

**32** Fact or Opinion

Maps tell you where roads and lakes are.

**27** Fact or Opinion

Some movies are rated PG-13.

**33** Fact or Opinion

Math is easier than science.

**28** Fact or Opinion

Horseback riding is the best sport.

**34** Fact or Opinion

Baseball mitts are made from leather.

**29** Fact or Opinion

When it is winter in the United States, it is summer in Australia.

**35** Fact or Opinion

Construction workers wear helmets for protection.

**30** Fact or Opinion

It is faster to fly than to sail to Europe.

**36** Fact or Opinion

Sailboats are more fun than kayaks.

**37** Fact or Opinion

Camels are used to cross the desert.

**38** Fact or Opinion

Sneakers look cooler than sandals.

**39** Fact or Opinion

It is healthy not to be overweight.

**40** Fact or Opinion

Male teachers are stricter than female teachers.

**41** Fact or Opinion

Lakes are colder to swim in than swimming pools.

**42** Fact or Opinion

Ocean tides change every day.

**43** Fact or Opinion

Cats are better pets than dogs.

**44** Fact or Opinion

Everybody loves peanut butter.

**45** Fact or Opinion

You can't see the stars every night.

**46** Fact or Opinion

The sun is in the sky even when it's cloudy.

**47** Fact or Opinion

Vanilla ice cream tastes better than chocolate.

**48** Fact or Opinion

Oranges contain vitamin C.

# |R|E|A|D|I|N|G|

## (Reading Between the Lines)

> **Players try to figure out the word riddle on a card.**

## Objective

To enhance students' ability to make inferences, draw conclusions, and make sense of abstract information

## Players

2 to 4 players or teams

## You'll Need

- Reading Between the Lines cards (pages 36–41)

## How to Play

**1.** Shuffle the "Reading Between the Lines" cards and stack them facedown between the players.

**2.** Players take turns picking a card from the pile. On each turn, a player shows the card to the other players, then tries to figure out what the word riddle says. For example, the name of this game (|R|E|A|D|I|N|G|) translates to "reading between the lines."

**3.** If the player answers correctly, he keeps the card. If not, the next player can try to guess the answer. If she answers correctly, she keeps the card and takes another turn.

**4.** Continue taking turns until no cards are left. Players then count how many cards they've collected. The player with the most cards at the end of the game wins.

**1** Reading Between the Lines

CL0headUDS

**5** Reading Between the Lines

MIL1LION

**2** Reading Between the Lines

DRESSES
SALE

**6** Reading Between the Lines

$\frac{1}{2}$ moon

**3** Reading Between the Lines

Hear ted

**7** Reading Between the Lines

N
W
O
R
G

**4** Reading Between the Lines

Geuss

**8** Reading Between the Lines

D
N
A
T
S

**9** Reading Between the Lines

sit

**13** Reading Between the Lines

HAND HAND CLOTHES

**10** Reading Between the Lines

?????
MY MIND

**14** Reading Between the Lines

SKATING
ICE

**11** Reading Between the Lines

House
Fire

**15** Reading Between the Lines

```
                    G    OCCASION
                N
            I
        S
    I
R
```

**12** Reading Between the Lines

CHAIR

**16** Reading Between the Lines

cake

**THE WEATHER**
**FEELING**

CANDLES
**Birthday Cake**

ZERO
**TEMPERATURE**

**SEC**

**OND**

**STUDYING A TEST**

MIND
MATTER

*Midnight*
*Going to Bed*

ENGAGE   MENT

## 25 Reading Between the Lines

MAN
BOARD

## 26 Reading Between the Lines

STA    TION

## 27 Reading Between the Lines

TALES

## 28 Reading Between the Lines

STAIRS

## 29 Reading Between the Lines

E
L    SAFETY
K    SAFETY
C    SAFETY
U    SAFETY
B

## 30 Reading Between the Lines

D A N C E    E
A              C
N              N
C              A
E C N A D    D

## 31 Reading Between the Lines

P p O p D

## 32 Reading Between the Lines

VISION
VISION

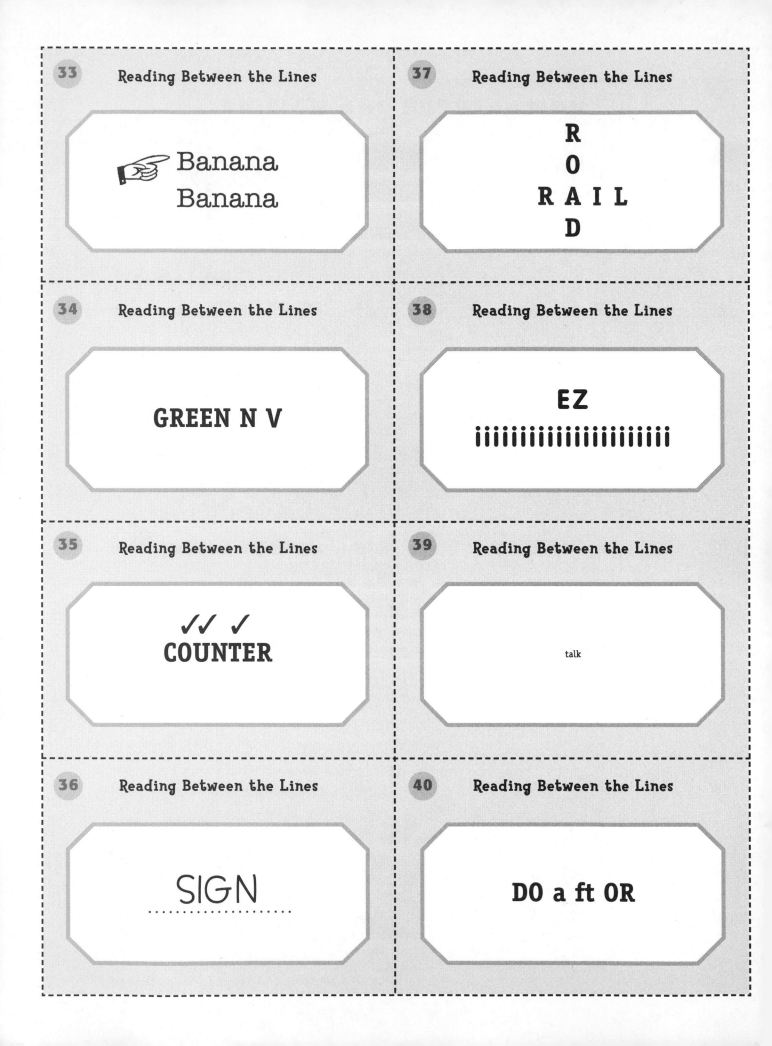

Banana
Banana

R
O
R A I L
D

GREEN N V

EZ
iiiiiiiiiiiiiiiiiiiiiii

✓✓ ✓
COUNTER

talk

SIGN
.................

DO a ft OR

HE'S HIMSELF

STEP
IT

SHOPPINGtoysBAG

NATURE NATURE

DAY **YESTERDAY**

HAYNEEDLESTACK

T
I
A
W

HAHANDND

# You've Got to Be Kidding!

> Given a sentence that doesn't make sense, players change the sentence so it makes sense.

## Objective

To help students recognize nonsense situations and use logical thinking to correct them; to develop accurate use of vocabulary

## Players

2 to 4 players or teams

## You'll Need

- You've Got to Be Kidding! Cards (pages 43–46)

## Optional Materials

- Game board (choose one from pages 64–67)
- Game markers (buttons or coins work well)
- Number cube (die)

## How to Play

1. Shuffle the "You've Got to Be Kidding!" cards and stack them facedown between the players.

2. Players take turns picking a card from the pile. On each turn, a player reads aloud the nonsensical sentence on the card. He then makes a new sentence that makes sense by replacing some of the words.

3. If the player answers correctly, he keeps the card. If not, the next player can try to correct the sentence. If she answers correctly, she keeps the card and takes another turn.

4. Continue taking turns until no cards are left. Players then count how many cards they've collected. The player with the most cards at the end of the game wins.

## Playing With a Game Board

Each player places a marker on START. Play the game as described above. If a player answers correctly, he rolls the number cube to see how many spaces to move along the board. If the player doesn't answer correctly, he cannot move. Place the used card in a discard pile. The first player to reach FINISH wins.

10 Critical Thinking Card Games    Scholastic Teaching Resources

**1** You've Got to Be Kidding!

Always put your shoes on before your socks.

**2** You've Got to Be Kidding!

The drugstore was out of cheese.

**3** You've Got to Be Kidding!

The florist told me to brush my teeth.

**4** You've Got to Be Kidding!

When I dropped the carton of eggs, the skins tore.

**5** You've Got to Be Kidding!

The car is almost out of gas so let's stop for a drink.

**6** You've Got to Be Kidding!

We climbed the tree with our roller skates on.

**7** You've Got to Be Kidding!

We had to blow on the iced tea to cool it off.

**8** You've Got to Be Kidding!

At school, the plumber taught the math lesson.

**9** You've Got to Be Kidding!

In the fall, the buds fall off the trees.

**10** You've Got to Be Kidding!

The kids watched the game on the radio.

**11** You've Got to Be Kidding!

James darkened the room with the new light bulb.

**12** You've Got to Be Kidding!

The mail carrier barked at the dog.

**13** You've Got to Be Kidding!

We dove into the pool from the oak tree.

**14** You've Got to Be Kidding!

The clouds are darkening, so let's go to the beach.

**15** You've Got to Be Kidding!

Sam painted a picture with ketchup.

**16** You've Got to Be Kidding!

The hardware store ran out of peaches.

**17** You've Got to Be Kidding!

Dad left the waitress a deck of cards after lunch.

**18** You've Got to Be Kidding!

We played catch with my yo-yo.

**19** You've Got to Be Kidding!

The words on the computer went from right to left.

**20** You've Got to Be Kidding!

I rubbed milk on my skin to prevent sunburn.

**21** You've Got to Be Kidding!

The air conditioner warmed up the room.

**22** You've Got to Be Kidding!

The camera bounced and rolled down the hill.

**23** You've Got to Be Kidding!

The house collapsed because it was tired.

**24** You've Got to Be Kidding!

My mother just celebrated her 15th birthday.

**25** You've Got to Be Kidding!

The dog and the goldfish played in the backyard.

**31** You've Got to Be Kidding!

Lilies and daisies grow on trees.

**26** You've Got to Be Kidding!

Dad gave me a ride to school in a tractor.

**32** You've Got to Be Kidding!

We put the baked potato into a glass.

**27** You've Got to Be Kidding!

We looked for the phone number in the thesaurus.

**33** You've Got to Be Kidding!

It was very funny when my brother fell off his bike.

**28** You've Got to Be Kidding!

The basketball team scored two touchdowns.

**34** You've Got to Be Kidding!

Horses can do cartwheels.

**29** You've Got to Be Kidding!

The President of the United States is elected every year.

**35** You've Got to Be Kidding!

The teacher wore ice skates to school.

**30** You've Got to Be Kidding!

We planted corn in December.

**36** You've Got to Be Kidding!

We took a big test during recess.

**37** You've Got to Be Kidding!

We bought jeans and T-shirts at the drugstore.

**38** You've Got to Be Kidding!

She wore shorts and sneakers to the school dance.

**39** You've Got to Be Kidding!

He tried to shave with a wrench.

**40** You've Got to Be Kidding!

She polished her nails with chicken soup.

**41** You've Got to Be Kidding!

When the alarm goes off, we go to sleep.

**42** You've Got to Be Kidding!

We like to eat cereal for dinner.

**43** You've Got to Be Kidding!

We spent our summer vacation at the library.

**44** You've Got to Be Kidding!

Thanksgiving is a great day at school.

**45** You've Got to Be Kidding!

A lake is as deep as the ocean.

**46** You've Got to Be Kidding!

We rowed our canoe in the ocean.

**47** You've Got to Be Kidding!

A sweater is as warm as a ski jacket.

**48** You've Got to Be Kidding!

Australia is just as near to the United States as Canada.

# Classified

## Players read and sort classified ads into categories.

## Objective

To give students practice sorting information into appropriate categories and making generalizations using real-life situations

## Players

2 to 4 players

## You'll Need

- Classified Ads cards (pages 48–51)
- Help Wanted chart (page 52), for each player
- Miscellaneous Ads chart (page 53), for each player

## How to Play

1. Shuffle the "Classified Ads" cards and stack them facedown between the players. Each player gets a copy of the Help Wanted chart and the Miscellaneous Ads chart.

2. Players take turns picking a card from the pile. On each turn, a player reads the card, decides in which category the card belongs, places the card on one of her charts, and shows the chart to the other players.

3. If the player places the card in the correct category, she gets to keep the card. If not, the next player can take the card and place it on one of his charts. If he puts it in the correct category, he can take another turn.

4. Players continue taking turns until no cards are left. Players then count how many cards they've collected. The player with the most cards at the end of the game wins.

## 1    Classified Ads

### WAIT/BAR/HOST STAFF

Busy waterfront restaurant now hiring wait staff and food runners. Fax resume to 555-4321

## 2    Classified Ads

### GERMAN SHEPHERD

Friendly, sweet, housebroken. Good with other animals. 60 lbs, 3 years old. Call 555-3300

## 3    Classified Ads

### MOTHER'S HELPER

2 school-age girls. Light housekeeping. Experience preferred. Fax resume 555-8479

## 4    Classified Ads

### ACTORS/MODELS

No experience necessary. All types and ages. For movies, commercials, music videos. FAX resume 555-2128

## 5    Classified Ads

### LARGE 1 BEDROOM APARTMENT

$700/month, plus utilities. Call 555-2233

## 6    Classified Ads

### FINEST SPORTS CAMP

For boys and girls 8–17. Skiing, skating, riding, tennis, hiking, swimming, excursions.

## 7    Classified Ads

### LEGAL SECRETARY

Experienced legal secretary for senior partner of mid-sized firm. Shorthand preferred. Fax resume 555-4640

## 8    Classified Ads

### LIVE-IN NANNY

Experience and references required. Care for 4- and 6-year-old. Cook for children, plus light housekeeping. Fax resume 555-8891

## 9    Classified Ads

### ADMINISTRATIVE ASSISTANT

Responsibilities include reception area tasks and office support. Computer literate, excellent interpersonal skills. Fax resume 555-9915

## 10    Classified Ads

### LEATHER LIVING ROOM SET

Never used. Still in original package. $1100. Call 555-5654

## 11    Classified Ads

### CAR FOR SALE

2-door, white with black leather interior. Excellent condition. Call 555-8135

## 12    Classified Ads

### CHIROPRACTOR

For back pain, neck pain, headaches. Accepts most major health insurance. Call 555-9777

## 13    Classified Ads

### TOWNHOUSE APARTMENT

Large 2 bedroom, 1 1/2 bath.
$800/month. Call 555-9187

## 14    Classified Ads

### PART-TIME TEACHERS

Looking for teachers with experience to teach grades 9–12. Test prep, SAT, and new SAT I.
Fax resume 555-6789

## 15    Classified Ads

### RECEPTIONIST/OFFICE ASSISTANT

For midtown law firm. Must have computer skills, MS Word, experience preferred.
Fax resume 555-1561

## 16    Classified Ads

### NANNY

Needed for working couple. Live-in. Top salary. Fax resume 555-1143

## 17    Classified Ads

### SAILING CAMP

Off Cape Cod. 8 weeks. Boys 7–16. Saltwater sailing, elementary to advanced extensive racing, overnight sailing expeditions.

## 18    Classified Ads

### BEACH HOUSE

Waterfront house with private beach and tennis court. Large living room and kitchen.
$500 including utilities. Call 555-1787

## 19    Classified Ads

### LINE COOKS & DISHWASHERS

Experience preferred. Apply in person at 200 Restaurant Lane. Fax resume 555-9391

## 20    Classified Ads

### PHOTO TECHNICIAN

Color slide lab seeks assistant for camera room and lab. Darkroom experience essential. Color printing helpful. Fax resume 555-3453

## 21    Classified Ads

### THEATER CAMP

Co-ed, ages 13–18. Musicals, drama, TV, modeling, dance. Daily classes. Seven productions.

## 22    Classified Ads

### ANTIQUE SCHOOL DESK

Solid oak, 50" x 32", 5 drawers. $150.
Call 555-0100

## 23    Classified Ads

### RESTAURANT $ALE$

Expanding restaurant group seeks special events sales specialist. Excellent base salary, commissions, benefits. Fax resume to 555-5555.

## 24    Classified Ads

### TUTORS

For grades K–12. Math, reading, writing, test prep. Masters degree in education preferred.
Fax resume 555-0098

## 25    Classified Ads

### COMPUTER SUPPORT TECH

Consulting firm seeks full-time technician to maintain, support, backup, upgrade office computers. Fax resume 555-7777

## 26    Classified Ads

### LOST

Large gray tabby cat, no collar. Near Main Street park. Call 555-2277

## 27    Classified Ads

### BROWNSTONE HOUSE

3 bedrooms, 2 baths, living room, dining room, full basement. No pets. $675/month. Call 555-6614

## 28    Classified Ads

### 4 ROOMS

Ideal for couple. 4-room apartment. Conveniently located near train station. $475/month, plus utilities. No pets. Call 555-5732

## 29    Classified Ads

### SOUS CHEF

Restaurant seeks versatile chef to take over kitchen. Fax resume 555-0123

## 30    Classified Ads

### TEACHER

NJ's largest private school has immediate opening for biology teacher. Fax resume 555-9876

## 31    Classified Ads

### MARKETING ASSOCIATE

Publisher seeks outgoing, proactive, people person. Background in sales or marketing. Fax resume 555-2666

## 32    Classified Ads

### HOUSEKEEPER/NANNY

To help stay-at-home mom with cleaning, cooking, errands, and childcare (6-, 4-, and 2-year-olds). Recent references. Fax resume 555-9990

## 33    Classified Ads

### GENERAL MANAGER

Fast-paced, casual fine dining restaurants seek senior-level management. Fax resume 555-1122

## 34    Classified Ads

### CHIHUAHUA

2 years old, house trained. Very playful and sweet. Call 555-0255

## 35    Classified Ads

### FURNITURE

Dining room, living room, sleeper, kitchen, desk, computer furniture. Call 555-5161

## 36    Classified Ads

### TENNIS ACADEMY

Co-ed 9–17. 19 courts. 1-, 2-, and 4-week sessions.

## 37 — Classified Ads

### BROWN/WHITE TABBY CAT

3 years old, friendly, excellent health. Needs quiet home as an only pet. Call 555-1199

## 38 — Classified Ads

### FLOOR MANAGER/MAITRE D'

For upscale restaurant. Service background & wine knowledge necessary. Fax resume 555-0102

## 39 — Classified Ads

### SCHOOL PRINCIPAL

Seeking a dynamic, experienced, and innovative leader for top high school. Must have exceptional skills in school leadership, supervision, evaluation, and more. Fax resume 555-2078

## 40 — Classified Ads

### MUSIC CAMP

In Massachusetts. Ages 11–18. Piano, strings, winds, and brass. Daily chamber music, private instrumental lessons, orchestra.

## 41 — Classified Ads

### WAREHOUSE SPACE

15,000 square feet. Call Commercial Real Estate at 555-6868

## 42 — Classified Ads

### LIFEGUARDS WANTED

Free training for summer job at pools and beaches. Must be at least 16 years old. Fax resume 555-3111

## 43 — Classified Ads

### BEDROOM SET

3 pieces. Vanity, dresser with mirror, headboard and frame. $80. Call 555-2778

## 44 — Classified Ads

### BABY-SITTER

Monday to Friday after school, 3–4 hours/day and school vacations. Must have own car. Fax resume and references 555-7890

## 45 — Classified Ads

### BOAT FOR SALE

42-foot houseboat. Live aboard. Many extras. Must see! Call 555-2960

## 46 — Classified Ads

### DINING ROOM SET

Antique white octagon table with leaf, 6 chairs, old gold seats, 7-foot hutch. $2,500. Call 555-2788

## 47 — Classified Ads

### DRIVERS

For early morning newspaper route. Must have own vehicle. Call 555-2773

## 48 — Classified Ads

### OFFICE SPACE

For medical use. 1,800 square feet. Call 555-7188

# Help Wanted Chart

| | |
|---|---|
| Restaurant | |
| Education | |
| Office Work | |
| Child Care | |
| Other | |

# Miscellaneous Ads Chart

| | |
|---|---|
| Pets | |
| Summer Camps | |
| Furniture for Sale | |
| Houses/ Apartments | |
| Other | |

# Making Connections

> **Players answer open-ended questions on a card.**

## Objective

To give students practice in making associations

## Players

2 to 4 players

## You'll Need

- Making Connections cards (pages 55–58)

## Optional Materials

- Game board (choose one from pages 64–67)
- Game markers (buttons or coins work well)
- Number cube (die)

## How to Play

1. Shuffle the "Making Connections" cards and stack them facedown between the players.

2. Players take turns picking a card from the pile. On each turn, a player reads aloud the question and gives an answer.

3. If the player answers correctly, she keeps the card. If not, the next player can try to guess the answer. If he answers correctly, he keeps the card and takes another turn.

4. Continue taking turns until no cards are left. Players then count how many cards they've collected. The player with the most cards at the end of the game wins.

## Playing With a Game Board

Each player places a marker on START. Play the game as described above. If a player answers correctly, he rolls the number cube to see how many spaces to move along the board. If the player doesn't answer correctly, he cannot move. Place the used card in a discard pile. The next player takes a turn. The first player to reach FINISH wins.

10 Critical Thinking Card Games    Scholastic Teaching Resources

**1**  Making Connections

What sings?

**2**  Making Connections

What lights up?

**3**  Making Connections

What roars?

**4**  Making Connections

What buzzes?

**5**  Making Connections

What hums?

**6**  Making Connections

What writes?

**7**  Making Connections

What flips?

**8**  Making Connections

What sticks?

**9**  Making Connections

What rustles?

**10**  Making Connections

What flies?

**11**  Making Connections

What pollinates?

**12**  Making Connections

What molts?

**13** Making Connections

What hops?

**14** Making Connections

What slithers?

**15** Making Connections

What hibernates?

**16** Making Connections

What prances?

**17** Making Connections

What bounces?

**18** Making Connections

What cuts?

**19** Making Connections

What breaks?

**20** Making Connections

What sizzles?

**21** Making Connections

What pops?

**22** Making Connections

What dings?

**23** Making Connections

What shines?

**24** Making Connections

What melts?

**25** Making Connections

What rings?

**26** Making Connections

What rips?

**27** Making Connections

What rolls?

**28** Making Connections

What burns?

**29** Making Connections

What hangs?

**30** Making Connections

What folds?

**31** Making Connections

What cleans?

**32** Making Connections

What whistles?

**33** Making Connections

What stretches?

**34** Making Connections

What flows?

**35** Making Connections

What screeches?

**36** Making Connections

What turns?

| | |
|---|---|
| **37** Making Connections<br><br>What stains? | **43** Making Connections<br><br>What floats? |
| **38** Making Connections<br><br>What quenches? | **44** Making Connections<br><br>What sways? |
| **39** Making Connections<br><br>What squeezes? | **45** Making Connections<br><br>What waves? |
| **40** Making Connections<br><br>What spans? | **46** Making Connections<br><br>What snaps? |
| **41** Making Connections<br><br>What freezes? | **47** Making Connections<br><br>What descends? |
| **42** Making Connections<br><br>What bends? | **48** Making Connections<br><br>What instructs? |

# Let's Compare

> Given two or more choices, players decide which choice best answers a question.

## Objective

To give students practice in identifying various characteristics, using logic, reasoning, and life experience

## Players

2 to 4 players

## You'll Need

- Let's Compare cards (pages 60–63)

## Optional Materials

- Game board (choose one from pages 64–67)
- Game markers (buttons or coins work well)
- Number cube (die)

## How to Play

1. Shuffle the "Let's Compare" cards and stack them facedown between the players.

2. Players take turns picking a card from the pile. On each turn, a player reads aloud the question and choices then gives his answer.

3. If the player answers correctly, he keeps the card. If not, place the card in a discard pile. The next player takes a turn.

4. Continue taking turns until no cards are left. Players then count how many cards they've collected. The player with the most cards at the end of the game wins.

## Playing With a Game Board

Each player places a marker on START. Play the game as described above. If a player answers correctly, he rolls the number cube to see how many spaces to move along the board. If the player doesn't answer correctly, he cannot move. Place the used card in the discard pile. The next player takes a turn. The first player to reach FINISH wins.

10 Critical Thinking Card Games    Scholastic Teaching Resources

**1** Let's Compare

**Which is bigger?**

a chain / a needle

**2** Let's Compare

**Which is colder?**

rain / snow

**3** Let's Compare

**Which is louder?**

a bell / a siren

**4** Let's Compare

**Which is longer?**

an arm / a leg

**5** Let's Compare

**Which is heavier?**

a chair / a table

**6** Let's Compare

**Which is thicker?**

slice of ham / slice of cheese

**7** Let's Compare

**Which is stronger?**

cardboard / wood

**8** Let's Compare

**Which costs more?**

yo-yo / skateboard

**9** Let's Compare

**Which is duller?**

a spatula / an axe

**10** Let's Compare

**Which is hotter?**

a light bulb / a flashlight

**11** Let's Compare

**Which is quieter?**

a bee / a car

**12** Let's Compare

**Which is cleaner?**

a towel / a rag

**13** Let's Compare

Which is softer?

leather / cloth

**14** Let's Compare

Which is wiser?

man / dog

**15** Let's Compare

Who is older?

grandpa / uncle

**16** Let's Compare

Which is warmer?

tent / cabin

**17** Let's Compare

Which is lighter?

a cloud / a kite

**18** Let's Compare

Which is quieter?

a bird / a murmur

**19** Let's Compare

Which is softest?

wood / book / cake

**20** Let's Compare

Which is hottest?

stove / bulb / hairdryer

**21** Let's Compare

Which is lightest?

pencil / book / stamp

**22** Let's Compare

Which is heaviest?

desk / lamp / book

**23** Let's Compare

Who is youngest?

boy / fireman / grandmother

**24** Let's Compare

Which is tallest?

tree / teacher / mailbox

**25** Let's Compare

**Which is fastest?**

car / ship / jet

**26** Let's Compare

**Which is sweetest?**

milk / cola / water

**27** Let's Compare

**Which is sharpest?**

scissors / needle / hammer

**28** Making Connections

**Which is fanciest?**

jeans / pajamas / dress

**29** Let's Compare

**Which is toughest?**

salad / carrots / meat

**30** Let's Compare

**Which is crispiest?**

chocolate / banana / cracker

**31** Let's Compare

**Which is roughest?**

sand / silk / skin

**32** Let's Compare

**Which is deepest?**

lake / ocean / river

**33** Let's Compare

**Which is cheapest?**

gum / socks / magazine

**34** Let's Compare

**Which is slowest?**

elephant / turtle / dog

**35** Let's Compare

**Which is thickest?**

piece of paper / slice of cheese
slice of bread

**36** Let's Compare

**Which is most transparent?**

tissue paper / waxed paper
plastic wrap

**37**     Let's Compare

Which is most brittle?

paper / cloth / autumn leaves

---

**38**     Let's Compare

Which floats best?

brick / plastic jug / key

---

**39**     Let's Compare

Which is lightest?

book / orange / pen / shoe

---

**40**     Let's Compare

Which is darkest?

noon / evening / midnight / dawn

---

**41**     Let's Compare

Which is saltiest?

cookie / apple / lettuce / pretzel

---

**42**     Let's Compare

Which is crispiest?

pea / egg / corn chip / grape

---

**43**     Let's Compare

Which is quietest?

library / gym / park / kitchen

---

**44**     Let's Compare

Who is oldest?

child / adult / teenager / baby

---

**45**     Let's Compare

Which is stickiest?

nuts / taffy / cheese / popcorn

---

**46**     Let's Compare

Which is fattest?

dog / raccoon / pig / cat

---

**47**     Let's Compare

Which is most ferocious?

seal / dog / skunk / leopard

---

**48**     Let's Compare

Which is most nutritious?

candy / broccoli / cookie / mint

START

THE CANDY STORE

Go back to START.

BUS STOP

SCHOOL BUS

Lose a turn.

Go ahead 2 spaces.

Go ahead 3 spaces.

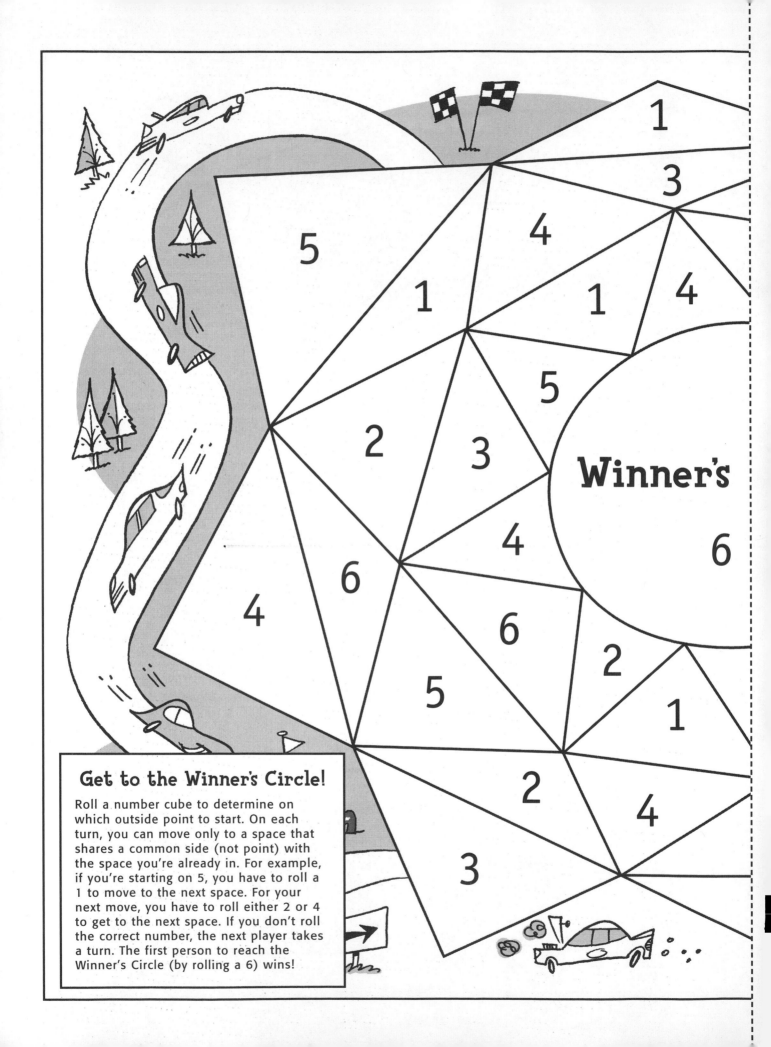

### Get to the Winner's Circle!

Roll a number cube to determine on which outside point to start. On each turn, you can move only to a space that shares a common side (not point) with the space you're already in. For example, if you're starting on 5, you have to roll a 1 to move to the next space. For your next move, you have to roll either 2 or 4 to get to the next space. If you don't roll the correct number, the next player takes a turn. The first person to reach the Winner's Circle (by rolling a 6) wins!

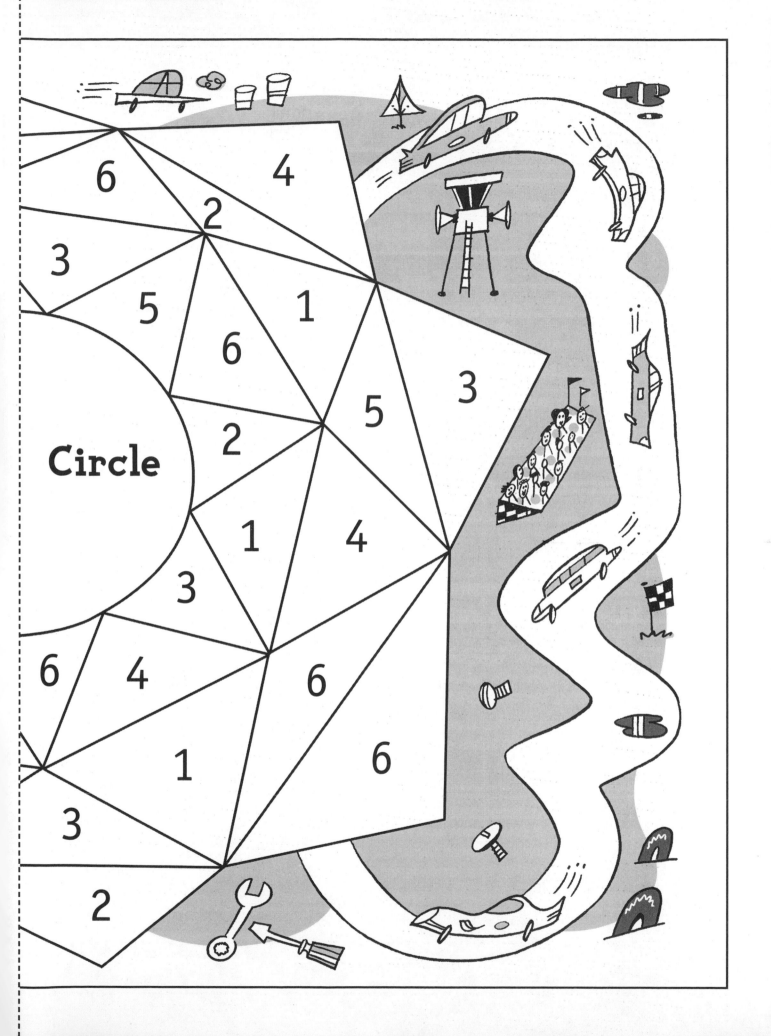

## Possible Answers    **Think About It**    (page 7)

1. Make a snowman, go skiing or sledding, wear a coat
2. They're both made of water.
3. Play the whole day, sleep late
4. Soup, ice cream, any drinks
5. Answers will vary.
6. Be born, turn 10 (or any number) years old
7. Fitness instructor, construction worker, life guard
8. CD, DVD
9. Doorway, pants, bed
10. Eyes, ears, clothes
11. Popcorn, coffee, vanilla
12. Book, pencil, bowl
13. Most fruits and vegetables
14. Answers will vary.
15. Water, clay, dough
16. Shirt, street
17. Truck, cargo ship
18. Canned goods, potatoes, milk carton
19. Reading, rock climbing, surgery

20. Meat, cookies, some vegetables
21. Clothes, seaweed, hair
22. Wool sweater, coat, shoes
23. Your name, phone number, address
24. Math facts, history dates
25. Love, friendship, happiness
26. Eat, cook
27. A doctor has a medical degree and can treat different illnesses; a nurse helps doctors and takes care of patients.
28. A computer can make superfast calculations.
29. A kitchen is a place where you can cook food; a dining room is a place where you usually eat food.
30. A peach is a round fruit covered with soft fuzz and with a large seed in its center; a banana is a long fruit with small seeds that you can eat.
31. Stew has sauce or gravy and different vegetables.
32. A person can talk, get his/her own food and drink.

33. A dog can smell and hear very well.
34. You can study many different subjects in college; a high school has a set number of subjects.
35. You can wear a watch; a clock is usually hung on the wall.
36. The President leads the armed forces of the United States.
37. A rose has thorns, and a daffodil doesn't.
38. Learning
39. Turtle, snail
40. In the city, near a hospital or firehouse
41. Screams, laughter, clicking of the chain
42. Cloud, smoke
43. Flossing cleans between your teeth; brushing cleans the surface of your teeth
44. Refrigerator, freezer, air conditioner
45. Your shadow
46. We need it to survive.
47. It can knock down buildings, flood towns, destroy crops, and so on.
48. Stars, lit-up street lamps or billboards

---

## Possible Answers    **Play Your Hunch**    (page 19)

Book – read, write, color, draw
Car – build, ride, wash, drive, fix
Elevator – ride, lift, carry
Hammer – build, fix
Stove – cook, fix
Paper – color, paint, write, draw
Pencil – color, write, draw
Pen – color, write, draw
Bowl – eat, wash
Pot – wash, cook
Stairs – stand, jump, sit on, climb
Cloth – sew, wash, tie, wear
Ball – play, sit on, lift, throw
Needle – sew
Soap – wash, smell
Coat – sew, wash, wear, carry
String – sew, play, tie, fix
Rope – jump, play, tie, climb, carry
Bricks – build, paint, carry
Spoon – eat, play, wash, cook
Backpack – lift, wear, carry
Bicycle – ride, wash, sit on, fix
Hat – lift, wear
Chair – sit on, paint, fix, climb

Pitcher – wash, lift
Button – sew
Desk – build, paint, read, write, draw, climb
Sofa – sit on, hide
Music – hear, play, dance, write, smile
Chalk – color, write, draw
Frog – hear, eat, jump, hop, cook, swim, climb
Tiger – hear, stand, eat, jump, roar, hunt, crawl, hide, climb, carry
Lion – hear, stand, eat, jump, roar, hunt, crawl, hide, smell, carry
Bear – hear, stand, eat, roar, hunt, play, hide, smell, swim, climb
Wolf – hear, stand, eat, jump, hunt, play, crawl, hide, smell, climb
Worm – crawl, hide, lift, climb
Artist – hear, play, color, dance, paint, read, write, talk, smile, draw
Pianist – hear, play, sit on, lift, write

Butterfly – build, fly, play, hide
Giraffe – stand, eat, play, lift
Monkey – hear, stand, eat, jump, hop, play, shout, dance, smell, smile, throw, climb, carry
Snake – eat, hunt, crawl, hide, smell, climb
Camel – stand, ride, sit on, lift, smell, carry
Flower – smell, wear
Fish – eat, hide, cook, swim
Boy – hear, stand, eat, jump, build, ride, hop, play, color, shout, wash, crawl, dance, hide, paint, smell, read, write, talk, swim, smile, draw, throw, climb, carry
Cow – hear, stand, eat, cook, carry
Horse – hear, stand, eat, jump, ride, play, wash, sit on, dance, lift, smell, swim, throw, carry
Shark – eat, hunt, smell, swim
Father – hear, stand, eat, jump, build, ride, roar, play, shout, drive, dance, hide, cook, lift, paint, smell, read, write, talk, swim, fix, smile, draw, throw, climb, carry

Kitten – hear, stand, eat, jump, hop, hunt, play, hide, climb
Canary – hear, eat, hop, fly, play
Dog – hear, stand, eat, jump, hop, play, crawl, hide, smell, swim, carry
Baby – hear, eat, play, shout, wash, crawl, smell, talk, smile, throw
Bee – hear, build, fly, dance, carry
Mosquito – hear, eat, fly
Sister – hear, stand, sew, eat, jump, build, hop, play, color, shout, wash, dance, hide, cook, lift, paint, smell, read, write, talk, wear, swim, fix, smile, draw, throw, climb, carry
Elephant – hear, stand, ride, wash, tie, sit on, lift, smell, swim, carry
Tree – stand, build, sit on, hide, climb
Onion – eat, cook, smell

68

1. The plant's leaves and stems are brown, withered, and droopy.

2. Some trees have fallen, some homes may have been damaged, houses and streets are flooded.

3. The baby is cranky or falling asleep.

4. The crackers are no longer crunchy.

5. When you cut through the meat, blood comes out.

6. The roses' buds have come out but they're tightly closed.

7. There's dust and dirt on the floor.

8. When you pour the soda, there are no bubbles.

9. The milk smells bad and little solid particles have formed.

10. Her face is puffy and she may look like she's in pain.

11. Some mold is growing on the cheese.

12. He was speeding and the police have pulled him over.

13. Mom is smiling, maybe even singing.

14. He is panting, short of breath, and maybe sweaty.

15. The car makes a sudden bump and is making an odd noise.

16. The soil is dry and the plant looks like it's starting to wither.

17. You see and smell smoke.

18. He is gesturing wildly and maybe yelling at the clerk.

19. The pencil's point is dull.

20. People are coming out of the gate.

21. The store's lights are out, and there are no people inside.

22. Your neighbor's mail and newspapers are piling up outside, the lights are out, you haven't seen your neighbor in a while.

23. Your best friend is sniffling, sneezing, or coughing.

24. The sun is very bright, or you might be going to the park or beach.

25. The peach is still a little greenish in color or it's very hard to the touch.

26. My face is covered with hair or the ends are scraggly.

27. Part of the hem is hanging unevenly.

28. There is a dent or a scratch on the car.

29. The picture may be somewhat blurry or the person's eyes were closed.

30. There are a lot of people over at the house and loud music is playing.

31. The bus drivers are picketing near the bus stop.

32. The weather forecaster said that snow is coming, or maybe the temperatures are below freezing and the sky is overcast.

33. The tree is very old and it looks like it's rotting.

34. Your mother has a huge smile on her face when she talks about you.

35. A birthday cake was brought over to her table, and her friends or family are singing "Happy Birthday!"

36. My shoes are old and have holes in them.

37. Your friend has a tan.

38. She's practicing on the piano or is carrying sheet music.

39. The road is slippery and has a thin, white layer.

40. The cookies are too hard or are slightly burnt.

41. You can smell the sulfur or see the smoke that came from lighting the match.

42. He smiles at you and talks to you.

43. Some of the paint is already peeling off.

44. You studied hard for the test and you knew most, if not all, of the answers.

45. The dog is barking and wagging its tail.

46. You feel very full, and your stomach looks bigger than usual.

47. Your clothes are smaller or you're closer to your mom or dad's height.

48. He's eating salads or other low-calorie foods.

## Possible Answers  Fact or Opinion  (page 30)

1. Fact
2. Fact
3. Fact
4. Opinion
5. Fact
6. Opinion
7. Fact
8. Fact
9. Opinion
10. Fact
11. Fact
12. Fact
13. Opinion
14. Opinion
15. Fact
16. Fact
17. Opinion
18. Opinion
19. Fact
20. Fact
21. Opinion
22. Opinion
23. Fact
24. Opinion
25. Fact
26. Fact
27. Fact
28. Opinion
29. Fact
30. Fact
31. Opinion
32. Fact
33. Opinion
34. Fact
35. Fact
36. Opinion
37. Fact
38. Opinion
39. Fact
40. Opinion
41. Fact
42. Fact
43. Opinion
44. Opinion
45. Fact
46. Fact
47. Opinion
48. Fact

## Possible Answers  |R|E|A|D|I|N|G|  (page 35)

1. Head in the clouds
2. Dresses on sale
3. Brokenhearted
4. Wrong guess
5. One in a million
6. Half moon
7. Grown up
8. Stand up
9. Sit down
10. Questions on my mind
11. House on fire
12. High chair
13. Second-hand clothes
14. Skating on thin ice
15. Rising to the occasion
16. Upside-down cake
17. Feeling under the weather
18. Temperature below zero
19. Studying before a test
20. Going to bed after midnight
21. Candles on a birthday cake
22. Split second
23. Mind over matter
24. Broken engagement
25. Man overboard
26. Station break
27. Tall tales
28. Downstairs
29. Buckle up for safety
30. Square dance
31. Two peas in a pod
32. Double vision
33. Top banana
34. Green with envy
35. Check-out counter
36. Sign on the dotted line
37. Railroad crossing
38. Easy on the eyes
39. Small talk
40. Get a foot in the door
41. He's beside himself
42. Toys in a shopping bag
43. Day before yesterday
44. Wait up
45. Step on it
46. Second nature
47. Needle in a haystack
48. Hand in hand

# You've Got to Be Kidding! (page 42)

1. Always put your socks on before your shoes.
2. The grocery store was out of cheese.
3. The dentist told me to brush my teeth.
4. When I dropped the carton of eggs, the shells broke.
5. The car is almost out of gas, let's stop for a refill.
6. We climbed the tree with our sneakers on.
7. We had to blow on the hot tea to cool it off.
8. At school, the teacher taught the math lesson.
9. In the fall, the leaves fall off the trees.
10. The kids watched the game on the TV.
11. James lit up the room with the new lightbulb.
12. The dog barked at the mail carrier.
13. We dove into the pool from the diving board.
14. The clouds are clearing, so let's go to the beach.
15. Sam painted a picture with watercolors.
16. The hardware store ran out of nails.
17. Dad left the waitress a tip after lunch.
18. We played catch with my ball.
19. The words on the computer went from left to right.
20. I rubbed sunscreen on my skin to prevent sunburn.
21. The air conditioner cooled the room.
22. The ball bounced and rolled down the hill.
23. The house collapsed because it was old.
24. My sister just celebrated her 15th birthday.
25. The dog and the cat played in the backyard.
26. Dad gave me a ride to school in a car.
27. We looked for the synonym in the thesaurus.
28. The football team scored two touchdowns.
29. The President of the United States is elected every four years.
30. We planted corn in the spring.
31. Apples and oranges grow on trees.
32. We put the baked potato on a plate.
33. It was awful when my brother fell off his bike.
34. Horses can jump fences.
35. The teacher wore boots to school.
36. We took a big test after recess.
37. We bought jeans and T-shirts at the department store.
38. She wore shorts and sneakers to the gym.
39. He tried to shave with a razor.
40. She polished her nails with nail polish.
41. When the alarm goes off, we wake up.
42. We like to eat cereal for breakfast.
43. We spent our summer vacation at camp.
44. Thanksgiving is a great day at home.
45. A lake is not as deep as the ocean.
46. We rowed our canoe in the lake.
47. A sweater is not as warm as a ski jacket.
48. Mexico is just as near to the United States as Canada.

# Classified (page 47)

1. Help Wanted/Restaurant
2. Miscellaneous Ads/Pets
3. Help Wanted/Child Care
4. Help Wanted/Other
5. Miscellaneous Ads/Houses/Apartments
6. Miscellaneous Ads/Summer Camps
7. Help Wanted/Office Work
8. Help Wanted/Child Care
9. Help Wanted/Office Work
10. Miscellaneous Ads/Furniture for Sale
11. Miscellaneous Ads/Other
12. Miscellaneous Ads/Other
13. Miscellaneous Ads/Houses/Apartments
14. Help Wanted/Education
15. Help Wanted/Office Work
16. Help Wanted/Child Care
17. Miscellaneous Ads/Summer Camps
18. Miscellaneous Ads/Houses/Apartments
19. Help Wanted/Restaurant
20. Help Wanted/Other
21. Miscellaneous Ads/Summer Camps
22. Miscellaneous Ads/Furniture for Sale
23. Help Wanted/Restaurant
24. Help Wanted/Education
25. Help Wanted/Office Work
26. Miscellaneous Ads/Pets
27. Miscellaneous Ads/Houses/Apartments
28. Miscellaneous Ads/Houses/Apartments
29. Help Wanted/Restaurant
30. Help Wanted/Education
31. Help Wanted/Office Work
32. Help Wanted/Child Care
33. Help Wanted/Restaurant
34. Miscellaneous Ads/Pets
35. Miscellaneous Ads/Furniture for Sale
36. Miscellaneous Ads/Summer Camps
37. Miscellaneous Ads/Pets
38. Help Wanted/Restaurant
39. Help Wanted/Education
40. Miscellaneous Ads/Summer Camps
41. Miscellaneous Ads/Other
42. Help Wanted/Other
43. Miscellaneous Ads/Furniture for Sale
44. Help Wanted/Child Care
45. Miscellaneous Ads/Other
46. Miscellaneous Ads/Furniture for Sale
47. Help Wanted/Other
48. Miscellaneous Ads/Other

# Making Connections (page 54)

1. Singer, bird
2. Fire, lightbulb, face
3. Lion, waterfall, bear
4. Bee, mosquito
5. Singer, machine, bee
6. Pen, pencil, author
7. Acrobat, gymnast, hair
8. Tape, glue, paste, Velcro
9. Leaves, branches, dress
10. Bird, time, airplane
11. Bee, butterfly, wind
12. Snake, lizard
13. Rabbit, kangaroo, child, flea
14. Snake
15. Bear, squirrel, fox
16. Deer, dancer
17. Ball, rubber, check
18. Knife, scissors
19. Glass, plate, heart
20. Steak, barbecue, food being cooked
21. Balloon, fireworks
22. Bell, timer
23. Glass, metal
24. Ice, ice cream
25. Telephone, doorbell
26. Cloth, paper
27. Ball, wheel
28. Fire, hot water, candle
29. Clothes, bat, picture
30. Clothes, paper, dough
31. Soap, water, cleanser
32. Train, whistle, teakettle
33. Dancer, elastic, rubber band
34. Water, river, syrup
35. Tire, screech owl
36. Wheel, car, world
37. Ketchup, grass, mud
38. Water, drink
39. Hand, snake
40. Bridge, year
41. Water, food
42. Body, river, bamboo
43. Boat, duck, coconut
44. Tree, grass, person
45. Hand, flag
46. Snapping turtle, duck
47. Stairs, elevator, escalator
48. Teacher, computer, book

# Let's Compare (page 59)

1. chain
2. snow
3. siren
4. leg
5. table
6. slice of ham
7. wood
8. skateboard
9. spatula
10. lightbulb
11. bee
12. towel
13. cloth
14. man
15. grandpa
16. cabin
17. cloud
18. murmur
19. cake
20. stove
21. stamp
22. desk
23. boy
24. tree
25. jet
26. cola
27. needle
28. dress
29. meat
30. cracker
31. sand
32. ocean
33. gum
34. turtle
35. slice of bread
36. plastic wrap
37. autumn leaves
38. plastic jug
39. pen
40. midnight
41. pretzel
42. corn chip
43. library
44. adult
45. taffy
46. pig
47. leopard
48. broccoli